Matthew J. Contrady

# Moving Magic: Moving with Children

Archway Publishing books may be ordered through booksellers or by contacting:

Archway Publishing
1663 Liberty Drive
Bloomington, IN 47403
www.archwaypublishing.com
844-669-3957

ISBN: 978-1-6657-5577-1 (sc)
978-1-6657-5578-8 (e)

Library of Congress Control Number: 2024901864

Print information available on the last page.

Archway Publishing rev. date:  02/15/2024

# acKNOWLeDGeMeNT

Thank you to all of the truck drivers out there that make moving possible.

Special Thank You to:

Alexis, Matthew, Bernadette, and Mikal.

Your support and patience must be recognized!

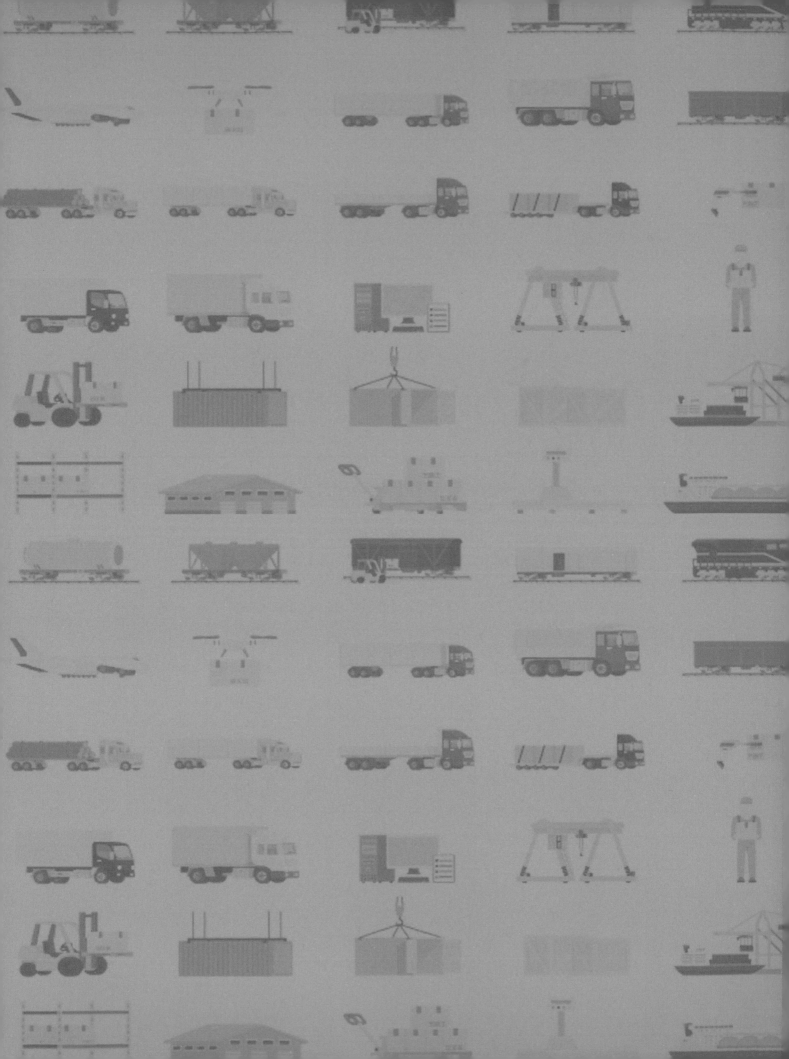

# Moving Magic:

## a Kid's Guide to a New Home

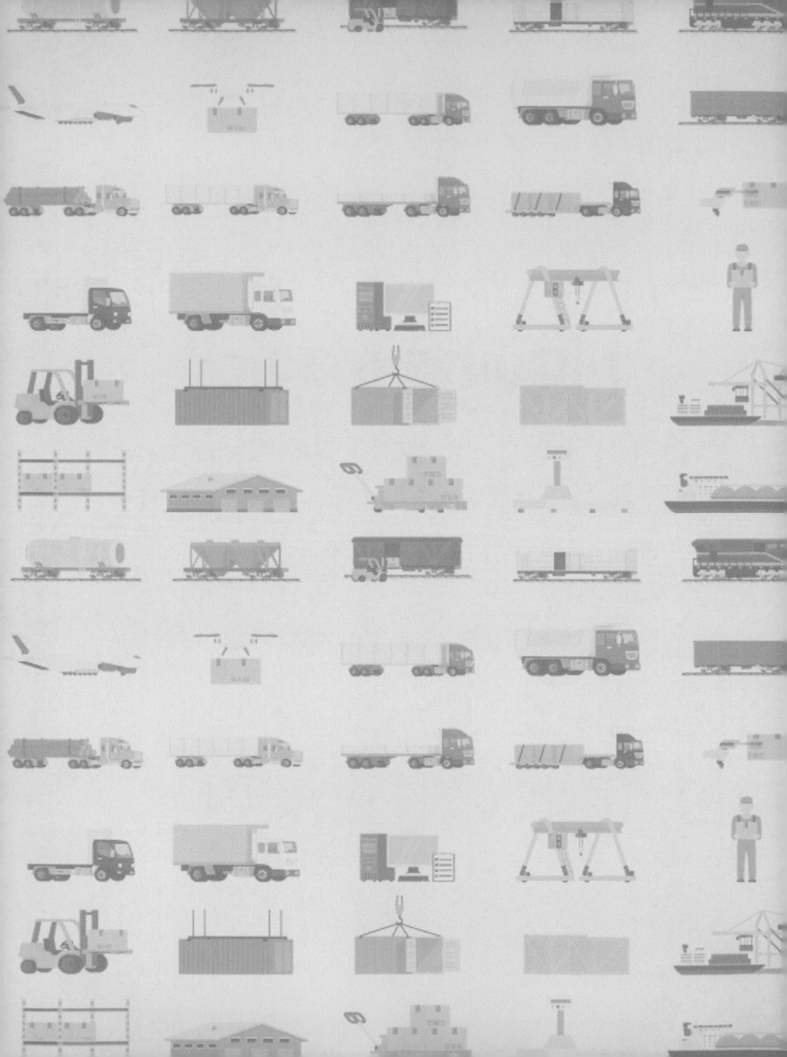

This book is dedicated to all the
adventurous families preparing for a new journey.
May your move be filled with excitement,
new memories, and joy.


Together as a family,
turn this move into an exciting adventure.
Enjoy every page together!

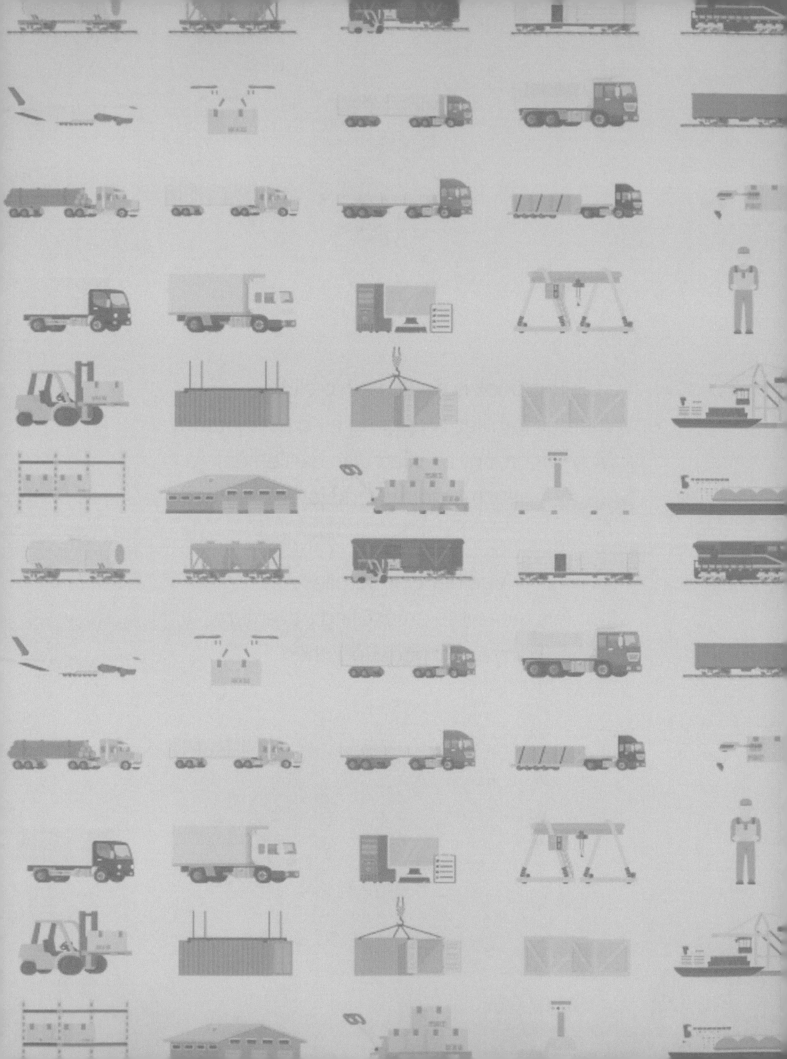

# Garage Sale

## How Can I Help?.

Checklist:

- [ ] Help with labeling items for the sale.

- [ ] Organize items into categories.

- [ ] Place price stickers on items.

- [ ] Set up tables and items for the garage sale.

- [ ] Help close the sales.

- [ ] Set up a lemonade stand.

- [ ] Sell water bottles and ice creams.

# New first Day Box

Activity: What will you put in your First Day Box for our new home?
(Example: Special items, pictures, gaming electronics, sports equipment etc.)

_____

_____

_____

_____

_____

_____

_____

_____

_____

_____

_____

_____

# Draw Your Journey

Instructions: Draw a picture of our current home and what you imagine our new home will look like.

# Moving Word Puzzle

Find the following words: **Box, Tape, Move, Mover, Home, Loading, Truck, Markers,** and **Boxes.**

| M | B | O | X | W | G | Z | D | L | K | N |
|---|---|---|---|---|---|---|---|---|---|---|
| C | R | F | D | M | M | H | G | O | R | B |
| T | D | M | V | O | B | O | J | A | U | P |
| A | A | O | Y | V | W | M | S | D | L | K |
| P | T | V | H | E | R | E | R | I | D | G |
| E | G | E | K | R | Y | H | G | N | A | B |
| Q | H | J | P | B | F | T | I | G | C | Q |
| D | I | N | T | R | U | C | K | Z | Y | T |
| F | U | M | Y | W | D | Z | H | D | G | U |
| J | L | H | S | M | A | R | K | E | R | S |
| B | O | X | E | S | W | J | S | V | Z | X |

# Crossword Puzzle

ACROSS

1) What is happening
2) Used to seal boxes
3) Used to write on boxes
4) Things get pack in

Activity:

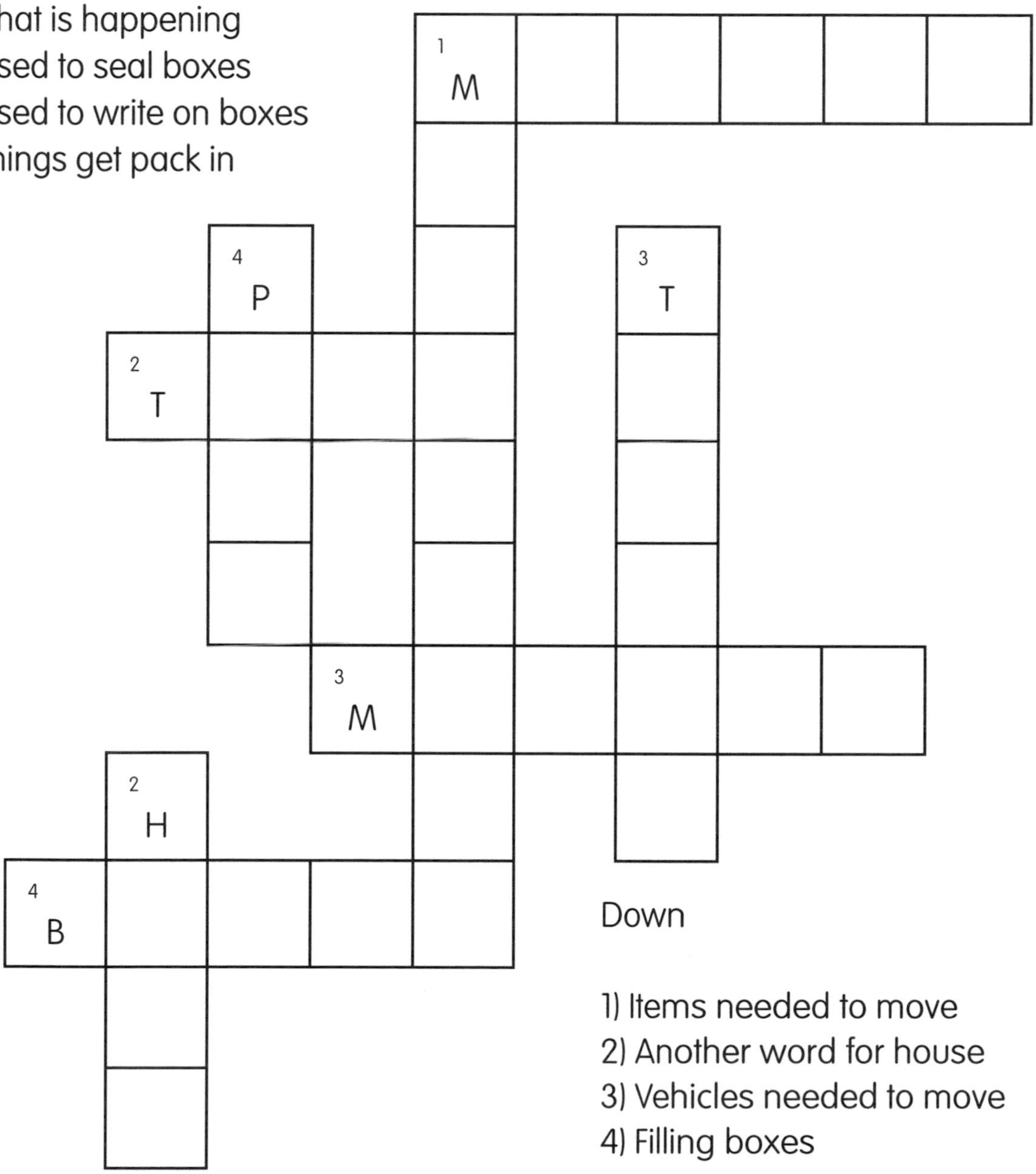


Down

1) Items needed to move
2) Another word for house
3) Vehicles needed to move
4) Filling boxes

# Box Sorting Word Match

Activity: A matching game in which children decide what items
go in small, medium, large, fragile, and wardrobe boxes.

These drafts aim to make the moving process engaging and educational for children.

Small

_____

_____

Medium

_____

_____

Large

_____

_____

Dish packs

_____
_____
_____
_____

Wardrobe

_____
_____
_____
_____

# Types of Moving Trucks

Activity: Draw and color different types of moving trucks such as small trucks, tractor trailers, and car carriers.

# New address Labels

Name:

New Address:

Name:

New Address:

Name:

New Address:

Name:

New Address:

Name:

New Address:

Name:

New Address:

Name:

New Address:

Name:

New Address:

# autographs

# Messages

| | B | O | X | | | | L | | | |
|---|---|---|---|---|---|---|---|---|---|---|
| | | | | M | | H | | O | | |
| T | | M | | O | | O | | A | | |
| A | | O | | V | | M | | D | | |
| P | | V | | E | | E | | I | | |
| E | | E | | R | | | | N | | |
| | | | | | | | | G | | |
| | | | T | R | U | C | K | | | |
| | | | | | | | | | | |
| | | | | M | A | R | K | E | R | S |
| B | O | X | E | S | | | | | | |

# ANSWER:

```
              ¹M  O  V  I  N  G
               A
       ⁴P     ³T         ³T
  ²T  A  P  E             R
       C     R           U
       K     I           C
         ³M  A  R  K  E  R
  ²H        L           S
⁴B  O  X  E  S
   M
   E
```

13

Printed in the United States
by Baker & Taylor Publisher Services